The Secret Powers of Naming

the secret powers of naming

Sara Littlecrow-Russell

With an introduction by Joy Harjo

The University of Arizona Press Tucson

The University of Arizona Press
© 2006 Sara Littlecrow-Russell

www.uapress.arizona.edu

Library of Congress Cataloging-in-Publication Data
appear on the last printed page of this book.

Publication of this book is made possible in part by
the proceeds of a permanent endowment created with
the assistance of a Challenge Grant from the National
Endowment for the Humanities, a federal agency.

Manufactured in the United States of America on acid-
free, archival-quality paper.

13 12 11 10 09 08   7 6 5 4 3 2

Contents

Introduction

Joy Harjo

This first book by Sara Littlecrow-Russell counters the tourist images of Indians as only colorful dancers, stoic saints, defeated warriors, or luscious princesses with a little truth telling, sarcasm, and humor. She upsets the status quo. These are not poems constructed of beautiful images, nor are they poems of redemption. There is scarce mystical panache. What you will find is a hard-hitting, wise witness to these times at the beginning of the 21st century here in Indian country, where everything is as it seems, no matter how outrageous. There is no magical realism here: we are human beings in the rough who manage to shine once in awhile in the light of self-deprecating humor as we dance colorfully or act out the soap opera of stoic saints, defeated warriors, and luscious princesses.

These poems emerge from the tradition of truth tellers: Littlecrow-Russell stands within a tradition of truth tellers who witness from the middle of the square, the plaza, the center of the encampment. Her poems are short quips, snaps of lyrics and voice, more compact than the long, eloquent speeches given at crucial historical events. The intent is the same: to stand with dignity, to help make sense in a world that has been severed from its moorings: from the earth and sky. These words are from the heart of the collection, from her poem "Invisible Indians":

"Let's run away," I said.
So we huddled in the frozen alleyway
Sharing my last cigarette
As fluorescent lights drained
The spirit from our skin,
Making us nameless, invisible.

After work, we took a shortcut
Through the predatory darkness of the park—
Frozen grass crunching
Was the closest way home.

Soft wings whooshed over our heads
As an owl shattered
Brittle moonlight of urban winter
With the power of naming,

"Ko-ko-ko!"

We lifted our arms in greeting,

And then she comes back around with more heartfelt
tribute, gossip talk and innuendo, bawdy humor, and
sarcasm, with another round of painful witnessing.

The power of naming forms the crux of meaning here
in these poems. To give a name, to be named, sets up a
relationship, a connection, makes a community of sense
that will stand no matter the tests of the unreasonable. A
name fires through the heart of the mess. Each of these

poems is, in essence, a naming ritual, gives name to a moment, an emotional field, a realization.

In this collection I am reminded of the poetry of nila northSun, of her classic *diet pepsi & nacho cheese*. I can also detect the influences of the poetry of Anishinabe poet Diane Burns, Geary Hobson (Chickasaw), and Roque Dalton, the Salvadoran poet.

Agitation is good, Dick Gregory was heard to say during the civil rights struggles of the sixties and seventies, it knocks loose the debris of the wreck. Those aren't his words exactly, but the core of the sentiment is at work here in these poems. We don't really come to know who we are as individuals, members of our families, tribal nations, or countries until we are tested. What you find here in these pages might test you, agitate you, make you weep or laugh, and probably everything, all at the same time. The voice you will hear when you open these pages is genuine, provocative. If anything, maybe the book will stem the flood of "wanna-be" Indians, those who are in love with the invention of Indians, the idea of Indian. If so, that's worth the price.

Author's Statement: The Secret Powers of Naming

All things that are natural are shaped like a circle, this book
included. Although each poem is linked to the next in a circular
journey of naming, it is not in the holistic flow of the seasons
and stars. It is a methodical walk around the chamber of a
revolver loaded with five colonial bullets. The bullets are alcohol,
disease, poverty, violence, and assimilation. This book is named
these things because the sacred act of naming brings power over
them. The sixth, empty chamber of the gun is named "survival."
In English, survival is a noun. It is static. It can be owned.
Bought. Sold. Traded. In my *Concise Dictionary of Minnesota
Ojibway,* "survival" is a verb. An act of motion. A choice of
direction. It cannot be owned, it must be lived. The verb is
zhaabwii—loosely translated as "the act of passing through
intact." This book is the search for the spiritual and political
power of *zhaabwii.* The true name of survival.

The Secret Powers of Naming

Evening in a Northern Kitchen

Coffee from old pots and pans
Tastes like tinfoil and loose fillings.
Raw beef kidneys are like gamy jello,
But melted, stolen candy bars
Are sweet as the tiny wild berries
Growing between rusty soda cans.

Horse shit on work boots
Dances aromatic smoke-spirals
With sweet grass and dollar cigarettes,
Awakening sweat-stained star blankets
Musty memories of skin
Hovering hungrily near the iron stove
Where impatient commodity beans bubble
And the broken deer spills languidly
Across the rough pine floor—
Metallic smell of death,
Crushed fender cooling in the yard.

The New Buffalo

Politicians and tribal leaders
Sit under New Buffalo courting robes
To flirt and sign Gaming Compacts
While coyotes eagerly dig
Through stinking piles
Of brown Taino flesh
Searching for the severed hands
That could not provide
Enough Indian gold
The first time . . .

Indian Ruins

"I want to see Indian ruins."

So I drove him
Past HUD houses and boarded trailers,
Beer bottles and blood drops,
And a three-year-old girl huffing glue
From a brown paper bag.

We came to a place
Where the earth lay torn and scarred,
Littered with shards of pottery
And bits of ancestral bone.
"At last," he exclaimed,
"Real Indian ruins!"

Flyer on My Windshield Announces the Opening of the 1999–2000 Indian Hunting Season

Dear South Dakota Hunters:
As the Indians need to be thinned out every 2–3 years,
This year, we will have open season
For the species Americanus Worthless Slounis Pyutus
Commonly known as "Prairie Niggers."

Regulations
In the 1999–2000 season, it is unlawful to:
Hunt in a party of more than 150 persons,
Use more than 35 rabid hunting dogs,
Shoot in a public tavern
(bullet may ricochet and hit white people),
Shoot an Indian sleeping on a sidewalk,
Shoot length-wise in a welfare line.

No traps within 15 feet of a liquor store
Traps may not be baited
With Muscatel, Lysol, or rubbing alcohol.

It is unlawful to possess a road-kill Indian,
However, special permits shall be issued to people
With semi-tractor trailers and one-ton pickup trucks.

With a road-kill permit in place,
You may bait the highway with food stamps.

Good hunting!

Escape from the Rez on a Saturday Night

You sit across from me
in a Tommy Hilfiger half-shirt
and great-grandma's beaded barrette.

"This sucks, there's nothing to do."

Your lipsticky mouth
takes a drag off your stolen cigarette,
as you get up to dance.

Skin-tight bellbottoms
strain against the muscles
of your Iroquois Smoke Dancer's legs—
10,000-year-old rhythm collides
with hardcore hip-hop thunder.
You dance hard in a world
that does not welcome you as Indian,
but loves a delectable 12-year-old girl.

All night I watch
the dopeman watching you,
because you just want
something happenin' around here.

Mourning Dove Dances

Hair cropped with dull scissors
You shuffled through the honor dance
Like a stroke victim.
We wept like the snow bank
Melting across the rust-brown smears
Of brain tissue in the parking lot
Where your husband was run over
And run over
And run over again
By men who still fight the Indian Wars.

You danced, we cried.
The tourists snapped their cameras
And reached out to run their hands
Over the beadwork on your dress.

Savage Romance

I was standing in the 90-degree sun
In 18 pounds of deerskin dress
Selling my husband's crafts
To tight-fisted tourists
When she pushed by me
To grab his arm.
"I want my next husband to be Indian!"
I thought about emptying
My water bottle onto her head
But figured I'd feel better
If I dumped it on my own.
I thought about grabbing her arm
And asking if she'd prefer an Indian wife,
Or offering Pepto Bismol
To help her digest her Harlequin romance novels.

Instead I offered my husband.

Is It Too Much to Ask?

Sitting on the bleachers,
We wash down frybread with Diet Pepsi,
Pretending we're watching the dancing.
So many beautiful men,
But in Ojibway there are many ways to say
Something is nice to look at
And it's not always a compliment.

A dancer with a bristling bustle of eagle feathers
Poses for the tourist's camera,
His hands subtly stroking a woman's
Sweaty, bare, white rolls of fat.

"He paid money for those eagle feathers."
I say under my breath.

You laugh.
"Ego feathers."

An intertribal is called,
The arena fills with men
Flashes of brown skin and strong legs,
The somber trade cloth of Traditional Dancers
The fluorescent whirl of the Fancy and Grass Dancers.

"Is it too much to ask?
An Indian man who's not a drug addict,
With half a brain or more,
A reasonable amount of teeth
And not young enough to be my kid
Or old enough to be my grandfather?"

You look at me like I've just asked
The dumbest question in powwow history,

"Of course it is."

The Worst Frybread

I make the worst frybread,
Lumpy and hard—
Good as fishing weights
Or for patching tires.

I always get the grease too hot or too cold
Dough burnt crispy on the outside
And oozing raw in the middle,
Or else flopping into a paper towel
Like a loon rescued from a tanker spill.

The only people who ask for my frybread
Are hockey players needing a puck
Or lacrosse players looking for a ball.
My friends avoid my dinner invitations
Until I tell them I'm making stir-fry.

My frybread is so famously bad
That no one ever asks me to cook for hours—
Arms and legs swelling in the heat of the stove
While grease needles my arms
Like a stampeding herd of horseflies.

Song from a Reedless Flute

You are beadwork woven by a broken Indian woman
That I mend with cautious, needle-pricked fingers.
You are raw sweetness of burning *chaga*
Scraping my lungs and startling tears.
You are the bear claw necklace
No longer caressing
The space between my breasts.
You are cigarettes
That I quit years ago,
But sometimes smoke anyways.

You are maple syrup on snow
Melting on my tongue
Until I ache from the cold.
You are the cedar tree
Sheltering my childhood
From unwanted caresses.
You are the star blanket
Sliding off the bed on autumnal nights.
You are a stubborn braid of *wiingashk*
That must be relit with a dozen matches
Before it releases thin streamers of sweetness.

You are the love song
Played on a reedless flute
That only spirits hear.

Shit Work

In a dream I am helping an old warrior
Walk into the woods to die
Peacefully as a gnarled brown leaf
Settling at the base of an old Maple.
As we walk, I can feel death begin
To wrap his frail body in its red blanket.

Then he tells me he needs to shit.

I kneel down and push my hands
Into the softness of earth,
Nails scraping like badger claws
As I dig a shallow pit
And help him balance at the edge.

I clean him with fresh leaves
And crumpled fast food napkins from my coat pocket.
The soiled paper flutters in my hands like prayer flags.
The old man smiles at me and whispers,
"Daughter, there is much honor in shit work."

Windigo Council

The last time we met,
You told me that I dance
Like the back end of a mule,
But you'd dance with me anyways
If I promised a two-step
When the corn turned green again.

Autumn harvest was your skull
Crushed like a Halloween pumpkin
In the basement of your burning house,
While the County Fire Department
Leaned against their trucks, smoking cigarettes,
Watching the evidence against your leaders
Billow across the reservation
Like a Windigo compelling
People to eat human flesh.

This summer I'll dance
A two-step without a partner
And everyone will laugh,
Except the Windigo.

Imitation Eagle Feathers

For $20.00
I can tie an imitation eagle feather in your hair
From a distance, no one would know,

For $10.00
I can sew a patch neatly embroidered in a Chinese factory
"Confederated Chapter—American Indian Movement,"

For $5.00
I can photograph you in a black angry hat and braids
Against a rented South Dakota landscape,

But feathers, patches, hats, and braids,
Fives, tens, fifties, hundreds,
Cannot make you a warrior.

A Mask of Razorblades and the Voice of the Rain

For Anna Mae Pictou-Aquash

Indian Country knows your story:
February 24th 1976, another AIM warrior
Found crumpled in the Dakota snow
Like the body of a reservation dog
Used for target practice.
The deliberate myopia of the coroner
Ignored the slippery dampness of brain
Oozing from the hole at the back of your skull—
Instead, ruling drunkenness and exposure.

For identification purposes
Your hands were severed
And sent to Washington—
Where the tips were skinned from your fingers
And dropped into plastic bags.

The man with raptor eyes
Did not come to your funeral
Instead he spent his 6½ prison years
Panning truth from a hemorrhage of rumors
Until FBI spelled Full Blooded Indian,
Spent 3½ outside years
Smelting whispered testimony and soldering facts
Until FBI spelled AIM
And he held a mask of razorblades in his hands.

When he wore the mask, the truth on his breath
Burst the bloated, decomposing belly of death—
Names of certain AIM leaders
Seeped like the thawing semen
Dripping from her body in the morgue
Snitch rumors, COINTELPRO, orders to execute,
Dripping
Dripping
Dripping
The Voice of the Rain whispered
Into the tape recorder strapped to his chest.

That December night, as he drove home
An unnaturally big owl
Spread slowly stiffening wings across the road.
Kneeling on the icy gravel
He spread shivering hands across
Your feathered blessing.

Indian Tears

Your voice lashed like the coat hangers
In your mission school childhood,
Words firing wildly
Like a cavalry pistol at the Last Stand.

When the chamber was empty,
I kissed away the salt
From 500 years of weeping
Until my lips were
A red clay riverbed,
Cracked and broken
Under a South Dakota sun.

Lost Bird

Broken Ojibwe was flint shards
Lighting ancestral tinders,
But you shook your head,
"I don't understand,"
You said in English.

Then, your eyes flared
With bewildered instinct—
Small animal wildness
Furiously scrabbling
Against the door
Of a forgotten box trap.

English Only

In a wrinkled voice,
Delicate as antique deerskin,
He names things into the ear
Of his dark-eyed granddaughter.

Ancient words slip from his tongue
Smooth as of desert sand
Until the child stamps her feet:

"Speak English Grandpa!"

His sudden silence
Wraps around them
Like a diseased trade blanket.

Devil's Lake

For Grandpa Bill

Your battered car is an old wild goose
Returning each season
To those ancestral wintering grounds,
Resting a moment,
Then whisping away,
A new bookcase, a patched roof—
Farewells to be discovered after sunrise,
As you ride winds of exhaust and burning oil
Onto the predawn highway.

Cancer in your hip
Steadily gnaws marrow from bone
As you press the accelerator,
Washing down morphine
With truck stop coffee.

We sigh in relief
Every time you call us collect
To joke and laugh
As we guess which rest area
Will end your relentless migration.

The Ancestors

Thunder of oncoming rain,
Dripping new blood stains
Crunching desert sage,
Marching chants of rage,
I hear their voices.

Pulsing double drum beat
Blasting sweat lodge heat,
Ancient brave-heart cries,
Mothers' lullabies,
I hear them calling.

Eagle's scream,
Holy man's dream,
Owl's silent flight,
Peyote's acrid bite.
Their whispers live on.

Her Baskets

Her baskets gape hungrily at passers
But only the old ones stop,
Touching her baskets like grandchildren,
Whispering *"Manidoowaadizi"*
And sadly patting the price tags.

"No one buys empty ones,"
Whispers the basketmaker
With silk-screened business cards
And a half-sold table of splintery wares.

Late in the afternoon,
She puts on fresh lipstick,
Silences her baskets
With handfuls of dried flowers.

Petals quiver with memories of blossoming breasts,
Seed chaff scatters wedding blanket ashes,
Leaves crackle into verdant dust
As baskets strain to breathe life
Into little handfuls of death.

Manidoowaadizi roughly translates as *"something inherently spiritual."*

24

A Good Woman

For Grandma Yvonne

She evaded Indian Health,
And the Department of Social Services
Pacing thirteen labors into the worn linoleum,
Raising ten children
In blazing migrant fields
And heatless urban tenements.

She mended torn flesh,
Skillfully and frequently
As mending Salvation Army castoffs.

After the arrests,
She pawned the furniture,
Stole the rent and the car,
Drove fourteen straight hours
With bail money folded neatly in her purse.
Every Saturday she smuggled
Steaks and cigarettes
And every Sunday she prayed
For good behavior and early parole.

It Was the Only Way to Make Tips

For my grandmother, Norah

Twisted feet plunge
Into Epsom-salted water
Blue veins laboring
Beneath rice-paper skin
As water softens toes
More corn and callous than flesh.

Bulbous orthopedic shoes
Cannot ease cocktail waitressing
In high-heeled shoes
Like standing on lit cigarettes
And smiling:

8 hours a day
48 hours a week
2,496 hours a year
20 years.

When I'm an Old Woman, I'll Be Damned if I Wear Purple

When I am an old woman
I'll be damned if I wear purple
Or red or green or black
In fact, I'll be damned
If I wear any clothing at all
Because I will be in bed
With my 23-year-old lover.

When I am an old woman
I'll teach my grandchildren
To swear in six different languages
And drink strong black coffee.
I'll get them tattoos for their birthdays
And sex toys for Christmas.

When I am an old woman
I will shoot Coke cans off my back fence
And spit in the eye of a politician
With flawless accuracy.

When I am an old woman
I will spend my social security money on bail,
Get arrested three times a month
(Mostly at political protests),
But sometimes because I won't turn down the stereo
Or because I am sunbathing nude on the lawn.

Organic Shit

He says it's okay,
Organic shit
Good medicine
Keeps his head together.

Sacred pipe in one hand
Pot pipe in the other,
He's a righteous brother
Talking shit
Smoking shit
Going nowhere
In a haze of
Burnt tradition
Burnt ambition
Burnt truth
Burnt vision
Burnt culture
Burnt children
Burnt dreams

Just another burnt fucking Indian.

A Good Night

It's been a good night.
Bill's girlfriend
Traded her body
To a white trucker
For a ten-dollar bill.

120 proof—
Two cans of Lysol.
185 proof—
A bottle of dime store cologne.
22 proof—
A quart of cheap red wine.

She is shrewd
In the mathematics
Of alcoholism.

It's been a good night.
There's enough money left
To buy a pack of cigarettes.

She mixes her cocktail
In an old bleach bottle
And they sit in silence
Staring at the creek,
Drinking and watching mosquitoes
Dance over the blackened water.

Russian Roulette, Indian Style

Russian Roulette
Indian style,
Is the spinning cylinder
Of a 500-year-old gun
With 5 out of 6 chambers loaded.

Each bullet
Has a different name—
Alcohol
Disease
Poverty
Violence
Assimilation

Survival is finding the name
Of the empty chamber.

To a Case Worker

I came into your office smiling—
Too clean, too friendly,
Neatly dressed.

Not one of the deserving poor
Who say "yes ma'am" and "please sir,"
Who bow their heads
To avoid looking you in the eye
And move quickly out of your way.

I refused your vocational training—
Two years and bottomless tax dollars
Teaching me to say
"You want fries with that?"

I wanted four-year college.

You told me,
Scholarship or not,
I had no business there
Then made a noose
Of vouchers and forms
Tightening it
Until my future
Lay suffocating
On your office floor.

Stop Welfare: The Middle Class Is Going Broke

Her shiny, white bumper is slashed
With a red bumpersticker,

"Stop Welfare: The Middle Class Is Going Broke."

I want to tell her
My $565 a month for two kids
Ain't got nothing
On $104.3 billion a year
Called Corporate Subsidies,
But her face is closed with hate
For her work,
For her greying hair,
For her daycare bills,
For my dirty car,
And my tired clothes.

I want to talk to her,
But she will never understand
That my $565 a month and two kids
Is not why her full-time job
Only pays half her bills.
So I sneak out with a marker
And write "Corporate" between
"Stop" and "Welfare,"
Then quickly drive away.

Miller Brewing Company Presents
Celebrations of Culture

Spokesman for the Miller Beer cultural festival
Tells me it will highlight
The contributions of Native American people,

So I ask him:
"We've already 'contributed'
Livers, kidneys, FAS children,
And thousands of nice cars
That actually ran well.

What else do you want?"

Invisible Indians

Loading boxes through the back door of 7-11,
I watched your shadow cringing around
Sale signs and customer irritation
That your soft Cree voice was hiding
In the cash register's beeping,
That your portage of their groceries
Across the counter was too slow.

"Let's run away," I said.
So we huddled in the frozen alleyway
Sharing my last cigarette
As fluorescent lights drained
The spirit from our skin,
Making us nameless, invisible.

After work, we took a shortcut
Through the predatory darkness of the park—
Frozen grass crunching
Was the closest way home.

Soft wings whooshed over our heads
As an owl shattered
Brittle moonlight of urban winter
With the power of naming,

"Ko-ko-ko!"

We lifted our arms in greeting,
Spoke our names,
And were visible again.

Indian Time

Sorry I can't take your call,
Leave your number
So I can get back to you,
At 3 A.M. from a place
Where my cell phone barely works
Because I run on Indian time
And if you don't know what that is,
Wait on the line.
Someone will explain it to you,
Some day.

Coming Home

Back in the city,
I put the kids to bed
And slide into a hot bath,
My hair releasing smoke from
Your woodstove, your cigarettes,
The burning sage of your prayers.

Wild mushroom smell of lovemaking
Floats up on the steam,
Sticking to slick pink bathroom tiles
As your kisses,
Sad like loon songs,
Sweet like maple sugar,
Eddy in whirlpool swirls against my skin,
Sliding with relentless clockwise delicacy
Into the darkness of an urban drain.

Drive-by

Sparrow shriveling on the tarmac,
I want to blow tobacco across your beak,
Wish you a good journey,
Sing you a prayer,
But there are strangers around.

They would not understand
And I might get arrested—
Crazy woman acting weird in the parking lot,
Or someone might come over
To have a free Native American spiritual experience,
So they can write a book
Revealing the mysterious secrets
Of Indian sparrow worship.

Instead, I pinch sage from the dashboard,
Crumble tobacco from the ashtray,
And drive over to you,
Surreptitiously opening the car door
To lay an offering at your head
Then revving a getaway
From my spiritual drive-by.

Apology to the Wasps

Terrorized by your stings,
I took out biochemical weapons
And blasted your nest
Like it was a third-world country.

I was the United States Air Force.
It felt good to be so powerful
Until I saw your family
Trailing shredded wings,
Staggering on disintegrating legs,
Trying desperately to save the eggs
You had stung to protect.

Supermarket Traitor

Unbleached canvas bags in hand,
I grasp a cart without wobbly wheels
And stride across the parking lot.
A woman with an ambitious goal:
Meat, milk, cereal, coffee, eggs, fruit—
My list in thirty minutes or less.

Entering the store, I am confronted
By a tower of perfect strawberries
My saliva fountains
Toward their crimson lusciousness,
But I have to ask,

"Are they union picked?"

The produce guy ignores me.
I ask again and he rolls his eyes,

"Jeez lady, I'm union.
Don't that make a difference?"

I want to say
"Yeah, you get bathrooms."
But my willpower collapses
From fragrant torture
And his irritated stare.

I put a pint of strawberries in my cart,
But I skip apples because Greenpeace says:
Avoid toxins—eat thick-skinned fruit.
Emaciated Indonesians,
Evicted like Irish potato farmers,
Stare at me from a yellow landslide
As I search fruitlessly
For bananas without DOLE stickers.

Next on my list is meat.

Chicken parts ooze through plastic
As I read the cartons,
Trying to forget the PETA flyers—
Drugs, disease, factory farming,
The mucosal terror of slaughterhouses.

Damn! Which cereal am I supposed to boycott?
Is Nestle bad and General Mills good
Or is it the other way around?

Oatmeal! There's a compromise.
Don't think about pesticides,
Or small farms swallowed alive
By large-scale oat-farming agribusiness.
Don't think about my karma
Making me come back as a cockroach.

Coffee, your third-world cash crop whoring
Wakes me each morning
More faithfully than a lover.
I don't want $3.59 to collapse
Your homeland economic system,
But I don't want caffeine withdrawal headaches.

A quart of milk from a BGH-inflated cow.

A dozen eggs from the battery farm
Where chickens live under 24-hour light
Until they lay themselves to death,
And their corpses are ground into chicken feed.

Insect, cow, and chicken,
Forgive me.
Farmworker and farmer,
Forgive me.
Trees and plants,

Forgive me.
Forgive me.
Forgive me.

I am too poor
To buy my food
In the health food store.

Indians from Outer Space

Blonde stranger approaches me . . .

"I know what happened
To all the peaceful Indians."
He says in a conspiratorial whisper.

"Yeah, me too," I say,
"They're all dead."

"No, they were taken away by aliens
To a 'peaceful Indian' planet."

Some folk will believe
Anything white people
Write about Indians.

Native American History Class

First day of class
My professor writes the name
Of He Whose Name Should Never Be Spoken
Across the chalkboard
In large block letters
Carefully articulating
Each syllable aloud.

I Will Take Anyone to Bed
(Poetically Speaking of Course)

I have made love with Pablo Neruda
On the heights of Machu Picchu
I flashed the tattoo on my thigh
And hitched a lowride with Luis Rodriguez
I have held Adrian Louis close
And danced a wild reservation two-step
Until beer cans and disposable diapers
Spun around us like stars.
I have surrendered to Leonel Rugama's
Burning adolescent heat
And caressed Roque Dalton
From a luxuriance of bed sheets and red wine.

I stayed up all night reading Sherman Alexie,
Nine months later, I gave birth to twin poems.

This lust is not heterosexual.
I devour Nikki Giovanni and Patricia Smith
Like Sao Tome chocolate.
I have been known to steal away for
An afternoon tryst with Julia de Burgos.
I wrap Nellie Wong around me like a silk robe.

Tonight, I have a date to share a steamy bath
With Linda Hogan and Joy Harjo
And it's gonna be gooooood . . .

For Roque Dalton

Screams and sirens fall like summer rain
Outside the broken screens.
I drag my mattress off the bed
To cure the insomnia of 2 A.M. gunshots.

My shadow in the window
Might be too tempting
So I light a tiny candle to read
Your poems that dodge bullets
By making slow love on the floor.

Salvadoran poet Roque Dalton believed that poets cannot remain on society's
sidelines. Despite repeated imprisonment and torture, he wrote 18 volumes of
poetry. Though he escaped two separate death sentences, he was executed at age
39 on May 10th, 1975.

FUCK

For Magdalena Gomez

The bookstore computer said
The Gary Soto book was in stock
So a clerk helped hunt the shelves.

It was not on the Latin American shelf,
The Native American shelf,
The poetry shelves,
The non-fiction case,
The towering fiction wall.

It was not even in the cookbooks.

An hour later it was found cowering
Amid the juice-sticky blocks
And Disney pop-ups
Of the children's section.

"Even children can understand his writing."
The clerk smiled apologetically.

This is why FUCK
Will appear
In all my books
At least once.

How I Became Puerto Rican

Thirteen years old,
Walking back from the store with Stacy,
Teasing each other about boys,
Sharing stolen candy.

A car stops.

Man jumps out screaming,
"Give me my wallet, you Puerto Rican whore!"
Stacy runs.
I can't move.
Fear is an old sock stuffed in my mouth.

He spits in my face.

Tobacco-smelling warmness
Slides down my cheek.
"Give me my fucking wallet!"

"I'm not Puerto Rican," I whisper.

Man jumps back in his car.
"Puerto Rican whore!
I'm gonna find you again
And kill you."

My Favorite Boatperson

I like her because
She knows how much
Space she takes up
And she never takes
My space either.

I like her because
She understands that
Weapons that kill Indians
Are not allowed in my house
When she visits, she leaves
Her six-pack and her white privilege
Outside the door.

I like her because
We can argue over
Lipstick and politics
With equal fervor.

I like her because
She studies Indian law
Arguing with her white family
Until they walk away in disgust
Then sweeps my floor
And helps butcher dinner.

When we go to Mystic, Connecticut
Where 750 Indians were burned alive
It is easy offer tobacco in front of her
Because I know
If she got off the boat in 1492
None of this shit
Would have happened in the first place.

My Books and Your White Women

When we are together
All things are fine
Indian man, Indian woman
You bring me meat—I cook it
And when our bellies are full
We wrap ourselves in your star blanket,
Feed juniper roots to the fire,
And listen to the coyotes
Chasing the evening train.

All things are good
Until that other world intrudes
With burdens heavy
As shopping malls on burial mounds.

Each time we hug
My books and your white women
Are between us.

Poem for a Beautiful Texan White Boy

I know that you
Would kiss like a lizard
Quick flickering of tongue
In my mouth
Then, jaws unhinging
You would
Swallow me whole
And sated,
Return to basking
In the desert sun.

I Know You Raped Her

I know you raped her
But I won't tell because
You are Indian,
She is white,
And no one would believe
The words of someone in-between.

I know you raped her
But I won't tell
Because I love your wife.
You'll drive thirteen hours
To bring her flowers
And rub her neck
When she is tired.

I know you raped her
But I won't tell
Because her husband will shoot you,
Your family will shoot him.
His family will kill,
And your family will kill,
Until everyone has their
Hair cut short in mourning.

I know you raped her
But I won't tell
Because I know
The coroner won't ask the police
How you tied a noose
With two broken arms
And stood on two broken legs
To hang yourself.

Eagle Feathers across a Crow Wing

Beneath wool blankets
Older and softer than grandmothers,
I brush my face against
The staccato lines of scars on your arms
That mark your flesh offerings
And kiss the Sun Dance scars on your chest
Gently gliding my lips and tongue
Over the deer-skin soft welts
Of your agonized prayers.

Then you gather me into your arms
Like eagle feathers sliding across a crow wing,
Old burns on your hands
Showering sparks in the darkness,
Igniting the sacred birchbark of our skin.

Graduation Day

"My son is going to be a lawyer!"
Her voice startles through the campus bookstore
Like a truckload of gravel
Dumped in the wrong driveway.

"I wanna law school tee shirt,
A pen, a mug, and a hat too.
I want one of everything
With this law school on it!"

Her crumpled hands
Push wads of tired dollars
Smelling of toilet cleaner and machine grease
Toward the smirking cashier.

New lawyer stands to the side,
Brown hands hidden in the pockets
Of his new Brooks Brothers suit.

"C'mon Mom," he says,
"It's time for you to get outta here."

Conversation with a New York Cabbie

I left behind one thousand poetry books
When I came to America
And I cried for each one
Like losing a relative.
For the first five years
The tears came every day,
Now, after twenty years,
I only cry about every three months.

The light changes
Manhattan blurs in a swirl of designer exhaust.
His eyes are the damp gray ashes
Of a hastily extinguished fire
As he looks in the rearview mirror
And sees that my eyes are also wet.

"You're a poet?" he says.

"I'm a lawyer," I reply.

Ashes become stern as dry cement.

"You're a poet."

Noble Savagery

I am afraid of super-size fries,
900 channel satellite TVs,
Slot machines,
And RVs parked at the powwow
Like circled wagons.

I am afraid of college degrees,
College debt,
Corporate employment,
And any debate
Where sovereignty is not a verb.

I am not afraid
To change the soiled bedsheets of the dying
But I am afraid of the grandmothers
Stacked in nursing homes
Like anonymous Indian dolls
In a Wal-Mart warehouse.

I am not afraid of the dark
But I am afraid of all-night pawnshops,
Blue lights in my rearview mirror,
And children who flinch from a hug.

I am not afraid of hot pink dreamcatchers
But I am afraid of tourist postcards—

Half-naked maidens with feathers in their hair,
Geronimo glaring at Edward Curtis,
Navajo women cheerfully sifting through burial ashes,
Horseback warrior slumped at the end of the trail.

I am not afraid of romantic novelists,
Degree-riddled anthropologists,
But I am terrified
Of anyone who is not noble,
Anyone who is not savage.

My First Suit

These papers are smooth
As her scalp between hairs
Scattered like old-growth trees
After the chemotherapy clear-cut.

These papers are happy
As the cozy expectation
Of her mother's baking—
Bannock and wild salmon
Marinated in lemon juice and dioxin.

These papers are my first lawsuit
Printed on Georgia Pacific paper
Fresh from the river outside her door.

Sue Indian

Court officer smiles wetly,
Anticipating a security search
Until I hand him my lawyer's card.

As he checks my ID
His scanning wand droops limply,
"You're an Indian, huh?"
He grumbles.

"Yeah, Sue Tribe."

These Days My Prayers Come Twenty to a Pack

For Jerry Dunson

I stopped carrying tobacco ties
The day the state trooper pulled me over
And slit my prayers with a razor blade
To make sure I was not smuggling drugs
Tied into one-inch squares of red cloth,
Dangling from my rearview mirror.

These days my prayers
Come twenty to a pack.
When I get pulled over
I can say "Would you like one?"
And the cop can say
"No thanks, I quit that years ago."

Prison Prayer

For Luis and Ramiro Rodriguez

I pray for you this night:
That your *carnales* watch your back
That the guards don't find
Your shiv or your dope
That you never end up
A snitch or a bitch
But that you never end up
Too hard to care.

I pray for you this night:
That your parole board believes you
That your social worker has nice legs
That you never run out of cigarettes
And the warden gives you a job in the kitchen.

I pray for you this night:
To have gentle dreams weekdays
And sexy dreams on weekends
Until your twenty years are done
And you make your return trip
To the barrio,
An anonymous ex-con—
As muscled and solitary
As a rooster trained to fight to the death

From 7,300 days in the weight room,
Moving uncertainly
Through sunlight unbroken
By chainlink fences and
The menacing shadows
Of the guard tower guns.

Eleven Minutes

For Gary Graham, executed in Texas on June 22, 2000,
at 8:49 p.m.

This cigarette is the prayer pipe
That offers tobacco for your journey
But only sacrifices eleven minutes of my life
Instead of the thousand minutes you smoked
To killing eighteen years of waiting,
Or the last one you smoked—
That you wanted to last for 18 years.

Stale smoke rushes through my lungs
Like potassium chloride in your veins
As I exhale the three minutes
When five guards strapped your arms,
Legs, and head to the gurney,
Needle skewering your vein at 8:41 pm,
Eight minutes of poisoned convulsions,
Your last scream:

"This is what happens to black men in America!"

Ghost Dance

Two hundred seventy
Ghost Dancers died dreaming
That humanity would drown
In a flood of White sins.

Then the renewed earth
Would reclaim city and town,
Leaving only Ghost Dancers
And those who lived by nature's laws.

History books say the threat is gone.
The Ghost Dance died with the ancestors—
Wovoka and his sacred dream
Were destroyed.

Each time it rains,
I go out to the sidewalk,
Where the tree roots
Have broken the concrete
Listening to the water's whispering:

"It is coming soon."

Double Lattes and Earthworms

Wrapped in pinstriped wool
And feeling like CEO's birthday present,
I rush to the train and stumble
Into a man buying a Wall Street Journal.
We exchange smiles, stammered apologies.
I like the unruly bit of hair
That falls across his forehead.
He likes my tailored suit.

Our smiles widen
But the 7:28 train is always on time
So I sling my law books over my shoulder
And scurry on like a good commuter.

Small worm shrivels
Against cold, dry cement.
I want to hurry on
Because there are more important things
But then I stumble again.

Turning back, I pick up the worm
And cradle it in my hand.
Wall Street Journal man catches up,
His invitation for a double latte at Starbucks
Dying in his mouth as he stares
At the ball of mucus and dirt
Curling back to life in my palm.

Lunch Hour

Lunch furlough done,
I toss sandwich crusts
To the pigeon scratching crumbs
With stumps of amputated toes,
And my Diet Coke money
To the man behind the wilted cardboard sign
"Hungry, homeless, Vietnam Veteran."

I don't want to look at him.
His face looks like a puffball mushroom
That's been stomped on for fun.

I'm wearing lipstick and a starched white shirt—
My 16th floor ID dangles around my neck
Like a noose with my photo on it.

He doesn't want to look at me either.

Neither of us wants to see another Indian looking back.

Tuna Fish and Bananas

For Jon Kidder

Every day I bring
Tunafish sandwiches and a banana to work,
Because the janitors are striking,
But I am wearing a management suit.

Every day I bring
Tunafish sandwiches and a banana to work,
Because the janitors are striking
And my boss said
"Cross the picket line
Or else . . ."

Every day I bring
Tunafish sandwiches and a banana to work,
Hiding them in air vents,
In trash cans,
Behind the receptionist's desk.

Pretty soon we're going to be
Begging the janitors to come back.

Letter to Human Resources

For Gwen and Kalamaokaina

Thank you for your interest in my resume
But I'm afraid I must decline your generous offer
To lap from the lake of corporate gravy
As it puddles around the drowning,
Decline the timely payment of bills,
A stove with four working burners,
A couch that doesn't erupt stuffing,
Sexy designer shoes,
Palm trees in February,
And a drive to work on heated leather.

Blame it on that crazy Hawaiian woman,
Who appeared at graduation in a party dress
But threw down her coolers
Of tropical flowers and raw fish
To rush to my side
In the administrative aftermath
After I "accidentally"
Burned the campus sweat lodge.

The one who held my shaking hand and told me,
"You know to fight their taking,
After you walk across that stage,
You must learn to fight their giving."

Wounded Knees

Friday afternoon on the subway
Man staggers over
Begging change
I dig in my pockets
But my last quarters were
My daughter's milk money.

Woman next to me hisses loud—

"You weren't gonna give him no money
You just wanna see a black man beg in front of you."

I hear her knees cracking—
Bent too long
For richer folks
With lighter skin.

I want to part the softness
Of my new winter coat
(bought with borrowed money
to beg for better work),
Roll up my pants
And rip scabs from my knees—
Letting blood flow
Across the floor of the train
Into a 500-year-old story-skin of pictographs:

12-year-old Chinese girls
Imported for the 1900s sex trade
Forced to their knees to suck
The unwashed phalluses of California miners,
Cheyenne grandmothers kneeling on the ground
Gathering wet fragments of their grandchildren's skulls
Playfully smashed by bored soldiers,
Puerto Rican mothers, knees bent on obstetrical tables
Begging that their ovaries be spared
The scalpel of Operation Bootstrap.

I want to bleed our collective histories at her feet
Until the steel wheels beneath us
Begin to skid and shriek—
"We all have wounded knees.
We all have wounded
Knees.
We all have
Wounded knees."

Glossary

carnales. Literally "of the flesh," meaning "brothers." Also an affectionate barrio term for close friends.

cedar. Several varieties of a resinous evergreen, all parts of which are medicinally and spiritually useful. A common wood for making flutes. Cedar is often burned in ceremonies for cleansing and protection.

COINTELPRO. A secret FBI counterintelligence program initiated in the 1970s to destroy the leadership of the American Indian Movement, the Black Panther Party, the Brown Berets, and other progressive groups.

Ghost Dance. By the late 1880s the Plains nations had lost 90 percent of their treaty lands. Laws had been enacted to systematically destroy the political, social, and spiritual lives of the People. Most of the Nations had been interned by force or coercion onto reservations. Many were sick and starving. A prophet named Wovoka shared the vision of the Ghost Dance—a peaceful ceremony, that if performed with sufficient devotion, would cause the Europeans to be swept away in a flood, after which the buffalo would be reborn and dead relatives would return home. The religion caught like a non-violent prairie fire across the Plains, but it was misinterpreted as an "Indian insurrection." More than 3,000 troops were sent to suppress the Ghost Dance. This brutal campaign culminated in the massacre of more than 300 Lakota at Wounded Knee Creek.

mission schools. Intended as a progressive alternative to the outright slaughter of Indians, these boarding schools were founded on the assimilationist conviction that killing the Indian was necessary to save the human. From the late 1800s to the 1970s, thousands of Indian children were removed (sometimes forcibly) from their families and tribes and virtually imprisoned in mission schools. There, they were frequently subjected to physical, emotional, mental, and sexual abuse—especially when they attempted to rebel against the harsh conditions of the schools or retain their culture in any way (e.g., speaking their own languages, wearing non-Christian religious items, etc.).

Operation Bootstrap. One of many governmental eugenics programs that ran from the 1930s to the late 1970s. These programs specifically targeted non-European women and low-income women for surgical sterilization, stripping the ovaries from literally thousands of women. Operation Bootstrap specifically targeted Puerto Rican women. The name refers to the saying "pull yourself up by your own bootstraps."

owl. Called Kokoko in Ojibway, the owl is closely associated with warnings of impending death, visits from the dead, and at times, even bringing death itself.

sage. A number of varieties of the mugwort family, burned in ceremonies for cleansing and purification.

shiv. A crude knife made from anything available (mirror shards, pieces of scrap metal, bolts, glass, etc.) by prison inmates who are unable to rely on the protection of the prison guards.

Sun Dance. A Plains religious ceremony where dedicated individuals take on a portion of humanity's suffering and provide support for the natural balance by enduring days of excruciating personal sacrifice.

Taíno Indians. A subgroup of the Arawakan Indians (a group of American Indians in northeastern South America) who inhabited the Greater Antilles (comprising Cuba, Jamaica, Haiti, the Dominican Republic, and Puerto Rico) and were the first to suffer the predations of Columbus.

wiingashk. The Ojibway word for sweetgrass, a vanilla-hay-scented grass that is burned in ceremonies to bring sweetness and blessings.

Acknowledgments

Deepest gratitude to the ones who have brought a thousand blessings to my life: Gitche-Manitou, Mom and Dad, my children—Skye Dolman and Cedar Robideaux, my loving partner—Matthew King, my dear friends—Mary Bombardier, Fred Bixby, Jim Lescault, Magdalena Gomez, Maria Luisa Arroyo, and my Ferocious Sistahs.

"*Gra agus solas*" to my indigenous cousins on the other side of the pond: Sonja and Che Torpey, Erin and Bryony Holden, Niall O'Floinn, Kevin and Eileen Hayes and their lovely family, the luminous folks of the Earth Wisdom Foundation.

I am extraordinarily blessed that three incredible artist-writers stepped forward to be the midwives of this book: my mentor and "Arts Mother" Magdalena Gomez (www.magdalenagomez.com), the incomparable Joy Harjo, and Diane Way—the Lakota Annie Oakley of political art. Extra-special thanks to Valerie Martinez for her brilliantly insightful editing skills.

Thank you to all the people who intentionally and unintentionally brought some of these poems to me: Badger Robideau and the Robideau family, Tom Ladoceur and the Eagle Sundance Society, Gwen and Kalamaokaina Niheau, Jon Kidder, Jerry Dunson, Jessica Gajarsa, James Luna, Judge Maze-Rothstein, Pamela Bridgewater, Harold Siva, Jane George, Dovie Thomason-Sickles, Natalie Owl, Nichole Curtis, Kim Tall Bear, Ronnileigh Goemann, Stef Archer, Dana Woodruff, Louis Neidorf, Keren Goldenberg, Jose Antonio Juarez, Peg Bad Warrior, the Department of Public Welfare, the New Mexico Highway Patrol, and the extraordinary anti-racist trainer-organizers from The People's Institute for Survival and Beyond.

About the Author

Sara Littlecrow-Russell is Metís, a sometime lawyer, and a professional mediator specializing in cross-culturally based conflict and anti-racist education. She holds a B.A. in Medical Anthropology from Hampshire College and a law degree from Northeastern School of Law. She currently works at the University of Massachusetts, Amherst.

Her poetry and articles appear in a wide variety of magazines and journals, including *Yellow Medicine River Review*, *Race Traitor*, *Red Ink*, *The Indigenous People's Journal of Law, Culture, & Resistance*, *The Massachusetts Review*, *American Indian Quarterly*, *Flyway: A Literary Review*, *Cream City Review*, *U.S. Latino Review*, *Lilies and Cannonballs*, *Blue Collar Review*, and *Hip Mama*. In 2004, she was a playwright for *"We Got Issues!"* which premiered on the main stage of the Apollo Theater in Harlem, New York. Her poems and articles are published in a variety of books and anthologies, including *Sister Nations: Native American Women Writing on Community*, *Within the Sacred Circle: The Indigenous Women's Healthcare Book*, the erotic anthology *Touched by Eros*, *Coloring Book: An Eclectic Anthology of Fiction and Poetry by Multicultural Writers*, and *Out of Line: Imaginative Writings on Peace and Justice*.

Her first book of poetry, *The Secret Powers of Naming*, was named outstanding book of 2007 by the Gustavus Meyers Center for the Study of Bigotry and Human Rights in North America. It also received a bronze medal from the Independent Publisher's Association and was a finalist for the PEN American Center's Beyond the Margins Award.

Library of Congress Cataloging-in-Publication Data

Littlecrow-Russell, Sara, 1969–
    The secret powers of naming / Sara Littlecrow-Russell ;
with an introduction by Joy Harjo.
        p. cm. — (Sun tracks ; v. 58)
      ISBN-13: 978-0-8165-2535-5 (pbk. : alk. paper)
      ISBN-10: 0-8165-2535-8 (pbk. : alk. paper)
      1. Indians of North America—Poetry. I. Title. II. Series.
    PS3612.I877S43 2006
    811'.6—dc22
                                    2006013492